Book of Bookmarks: Words of Faith

By Debi Joy Beakley

Printed by CreateSpace, An Amazon.com Company

Copyright © 2015 by Debi Joy Beakley

All rights reserved.

Scripture taken from the New King James Version

Copyright © by Thomas Nelson, Inc.

Used by permission. All rights reserved.

Dedicated to My Mom

Leta Brooks

Mom,

Only by your love, prayers, grace and mercy have I learned to walk with the Lord. I want to THANK YOU for always continuing to pray for me. Even in the foolish years of my youth when I called and demanded you quit praying because your prayers were messing up my life, you ignored me and never gave up.

Your daily prayers continue to help me grow. Now with words given by the Lord I am taking my turn to help others grow. Great will be your reward in heaven. Please know without your prayers there would be no books.

I am eternally grateful for the example you set.

Love, Debi

A Note to the Wonderful Members of Sam's Club in Vero Beach, Florida:

Thank you for your prayers offered on my behalf. As many of you know, I had planned an extensive trip to capture nature pictures for a book. Health situations canceled the trip. God was at my side and not only was I able to complete the first book, **Messages From a Still Small Voice**, but a growing experience happened during my seclusion and I was able to complete this book: **Book of Bookmarks: Words of Faith.**

I then started taking pictures from out my window photographing the only nature I could see. **Out My Window: Life within the Tree** was born, expected to be released in the Fall of 2015. For all of those who were offering heartfelt, across the country help for my trip: I hope the disappointment of not attaining the original planned book will be lessened by the three books which I was able to produce.

With deepest gratitude,

Debi

Introduction

Sharing is a favorite pastime of mine. Especially when it comes to tricks and tips. Another favorite activity is to keep growing in my walk with the Lord. Now how to put those two things together? I started asking the Lord how to find a way to keep sharing in a quick, easy, and lasting manner. That is when the Lord showed me He had already given me a way...through words.

At first, I thought He meant the words He was giving me as I made my way, very slowly, trying to complete the first book *Messages From a Still Small Voice.* Then He made it clear: the bookmark. I had forgotten all about the acrostic bookmark. I use it continually in my Bible but the significance of why and how it was created had been placed on the back burner in my mind.

A few years ago I was attending a women's group at High Point Community Church in Port Saint Lucie, Florida. During the year the ladies would attend several themed events. This one particular event was titled Peace: What Represents Peace to You. The object was to share a way you found Peace. Combining my love for reading and the helpfulness of having a bookmark, you guessed it: I took each lady a bookmark, with help from Lillian Jacobson who printed them, representing in words what Peace meant to me.

After that the Peace bookmark became a door opener as I witnessed; others seemed to want to continue sharing this simple word with such a powerful meaning.

The Book of Bookmarks: Words of Faith is meant to accomplish this mission, sharing in a quick, easy and lasting manner everyday words with Biblical emphasis.

My prayer for the reader is that the following words bring you comfort, inspiration and strength. I pray that you receive confirmation and revelation as to how much God cares about you.

If you find the bookmarks might be helpful in your personal growth or help open the door to your witnessing please know this book was meant to be formatted in such a manner as to allow the reader to tear and share the bookmarks.

There is a *Book of Bookmarks: Words of Faith "Tear and Share" Special Edition* which required a specialist printer. The spiral bound desk edition may be requested by emailing Godspencil@outlook.com .

Peace:

*P*raise

*E*xaltation

*A*doration

*C*ommunication

*E*ternity

"You will keep him in perfect peace, whose mind is stayed on You, because he trusts in You."   Isaiah 26:3

This was the original bookmark.

Peace:

*P*raise

*E*xaltation

*A*doration

*C*ommunication

*E*ternity

Isaiah 26:3

Notes

God *is:*

Goodness

Offering

Deliverance

"The rainbow shall be in the cloud, and I will look on it to remember the everlasting covenant between God and every living creature of all flesh that is on the earth." Genesis 9:16

God *is:*

Goodness

Offering

Deliverance

Genesis 9:16

Notes

Jesus *is:*

Just

Eternal

Sanctified

Undeserved

Salvation

"And she will bring forth a Son, and you shall call His name JESUS, for He will save His people from their sins." Matthew 1:21

Jesus *is:*

Just

Eternal

Sanctified

Undeserved

Salvation

Matthew 1:21

Notes_____

Jesus is the **Rock:**

Redeemer

Omniscient

Conqueror

King

"He is the Rock, His work is perfect; for all His ways are justice, a God of truth and without injustice; righteous and upright is He." Deuteronomy 32:4

Jesus is the **Rock:**

Redeemer

Omniscient

Conqueror

King

Deuteronomy 32:4

Notes

Our *Bible* is a:

Book of

Instruction

Bestows to all the path to

Life

Everlasting

"I entreated Your favor with my whole heart; be merciful to me according to Your word."
Psalm 119:58

Our *Bible* is a:

Book of

Instruction

Bestows to all the path to

Life

Everlasting

Psalm 119:58

Notes

Through the **Word** we:

Gain **W**isdom

Learn **O**bedience

Apply **R**espect

Acquire **D**iscipline

"Your word I have hidden in my heart, that I might not sin against You." Psalm 119:11

Through the **Word** we:

Gain **W**isdom

Learn **O**bedience

Apply **R**espect

Acquire **D**iscipline

Psalm 119:11

Notes

*Walk a **Path** of:*

Pleasing God

Adoring God

Trusting God

Hearing God

"There are those who rebel against the light; they do not know its ways nor abide in its paths." Job 24:13

---

*Walk a **Path** of:*

Pleasing God

Adoring God

Trusting God

Hearing God

Job 24:13

Notes

*Look at the **Sky** and know:*

***S**avior*

***K**eeping*

***Y**ou*

"There is no one like the God of Jeshurun, Who ride the heavens to help you, and in His excellency on the clouds." Deuteronomy 33:26

---

*Look at the **Sky** and know:*

***S**avior*

***K**eeping*

***Y**ou*

Deuteronomy 33:26

Notes

Would you like **Wisdom?**

Walk

In

Savior's

Domain

One

Moment at a time

"With Him are wisdom and strength, He has counsel and understanding."
Job 12:13

Would you like **Wisdom?**

Walk

In

Savior's

Domain

One

Moment at a time

Job 12:13

Notes_____

Meaning of **Serve:**

Selfless

Endeavors

Regarding

Virtuous

Expression

"I thank God, whom I serve with a pure conscience, as my forefathers did, as without ceasing I remember you in my prayers night and day…"
2 Timothy 1:3

Meaning of **Serve:**

Selfless

Endeavors

Regarding

Virtuous

Expression

2 Timothy 1:3

Notes

Bless *is to:*

Bestow

Love

Exalt

Sinners

Salvation

"Bless those who persecute you; bless and do not curse."
Romans 12:14

Bless *is to:*

Bestow

Love

Exalt

Sinners

Salvation

Romans 12:14

Notes

Grace is:

Giving

Respect

And

Compassion

Everywhere to everyone

"For the law was given through Moses, but grace and truth came through Jesus Christ." John 1:17

Grace is:

Giving

Respect

And

Compassion

Everywhere to everyone

John 1:17

Notes_____

Hope *is:*

H*umbly*

O*ffering*

P*rayer*

E*xpectantly*

"…who through Him believed in God, who raised Him from the dead and gave Him glory, so that your faith and hope are in God."
1 Peter 1:21

Hope *is:*

H*umbly*

O*ffering*

P*rayer*

E*xpectantly*

1 Peter 1:21

Notes

Faith:

Finally

Actively

Intentionally

Trusting

Him

"...through whom also we have access by faith into this grace in which we stand, and rejoice in hope of the glory of God." Romans 5:2

Faith:

Finally

Actively

Intentionally

Trusting

Him

Romans 5:2

Notes

When you **Ask** *you are:*

Always

Seeking

Knowledge

"And whatever we ask we receive from Him, because we keep His commandments and do those things that are pleasing in His sight."
1 John 3:22

When you **Ask** *you are:*

Always

Seeking

Knowledge

1 John 3:22

Notes

Heaven:

Holy

Emmanuel

Always

Visible

Everlasting

Nirvana

"For Christ has not entered the holy places made with hands, which are copies of the true, but into heaven itself, now to appear in the presence of God for us…" Hebrews 9:24

Heaven:

Holy

Emmanuel

Always

Visible

Everlasting

Nirvana

Hebrews 9:24

Notes

A ***Servant*** *is:*

A **S**elfless

Encourager

Rendering

Value

While **A**ttempting

New

Talents

"Make Your face shine upon Your servant, and teach me Your statutes." Psalm 119:135

Servant:

Selfless

Encourager

Rendering

Value

While

Attempting

New

Talents

Psalm 119:135

Notes

Pride *is not your friend:*

P*roblems*

R*ecognizing*

I*nsecure*

D*eranged*

E*gomania*

"The wicked in his proud countenance does not seek God; God is in none of his thoughts."
Psalm 10:4

Pride *is not your friend:*

P*roblems*

R*ecognizing*

I*nsecure*

D*eranged*

E*gomania*

Psalm 10:4

Notes

*T*rust *is:*

*T*rue

*R*eliance

*U*pon

*S*avior's

*T*iming

"As for God, His way is perfect; the word of the Lord is proven; He is a shield to all who trust in Him."
2 Samuel 22:31

---

*T*rust *is:*

*T*rue

*R*eliance

*U*pon

*S*avior's

*T*iming

2 Samuel 22:31

Notes

Clap *with thanksgiving:*

C*hains broken*

L*ife restored*

A*ddiction ended*

P*raise God*

"Oh, clap your hands, all you peoples! Shout to God with the voice of triumph!" Psalm 47:1

Clap *with thanksgiving:*

C*hains broken*

L*ife restored*

A*ddiction ended*

P*raise God*

Psalm 47:1

Notes

Sob:

Surrender

Obedience

Belief

"You have heard my voice: 'Do not hide Your ear from my sighing, from my cry for help.'" Lamentations 3:56

Sob:

Surrender

Obedience

Belief

Lamentations 3:56

Notes_____

First steps to **Grow:**

Get

Rid

Of

Whining

"...as newborn babes, desire the pure milk of the word, that you may grow thereby..." 1 Peter 2:2

First steps to **Grow:**

Get

Rid

Of

Whining

1 Peter 2:2

Notes

Grow in **Peace** through:

Prayer

Examination

Accountability

Compassion

Exaltation

"The Lord will fight for you, and you shall hold your peace." Exodus 14:14

Grow in **Peace** through:

Prayer

Examination

Accountability

Compassion

Exaltation

Exodus 14:14

Notes

When **Grown** *your faith is:*

G*iving*

R*ighteous*

O*bedient*

W*ise*

N*ever-ending*

"...but grow in the grace and knowledge of our Lord and Savior Jesus Christ." 2 Peter 3:18

When

Grown

your faith is:

G*iving*

R*ighteous*

O*bedient*

W*ise*

N*ever-ending*

2 Peter 3:18

Notes

Strive:

Surrender to God

Trust in God

Receive from God

Insight about God

Victory with God

Endure like God

"Strive to enter through the narrow gate, for many, I say to you, will seek to enter and will not be able."
Luke 13:24

Strive:

Surrender to God

Trust in God

Receive from God

Insight about God

Victory with God

Endure like God

Luke 13:24

Notes

When you ask **Why** you are:

Wanting to

Help

Yourself

"And why do we stand in jeopardy every hour?"
1Corinthians 15:30

When you ask **Why** you are:

Wanting to

Help

Yourself

1Corinthians 15:30

Notes

*With God **Now** means:*

Not

One

Worry

"Now therefore, I pray, if I have found grace in Your sight, show me now Your way, that I may know You and that I may find grace in Your sight. And consider that this nation is Your people." Exodus 33:13

With God

Now

means:

Not

One

Worry

Exodus 33:13

Notes

Christians who **Thrive** are:

Trusting

Helping

Reflecting

Inspiring

Victorious

Examples

"For I have given you an example, that you should do as I have done…"
John 13:15

Christians who **Thrive** are:

Trusting

Helping

Reflecting

Inspiring

Victorious

Examples

John 13:15

Notes

*It is important to **Rest:***

Relax

Experience

Serene

Tranquility

"For he who has entered His rest has himself also ceased from his works as God did from His." Hebrews 4:10

---

*It is important to **Rest:***

Relax

Experience

Serene

Tranquility

Hebrews 4:10

Notes

When you **Pray:**

Offer **P**raise

Make **R**equest

Listen for **A**nswer

Yield to God

"I desire therefore that the men pray everywhere, lifting up holy hands, without wrath and doubting..."
1 Timothy 2:8

When you **Pray:**

Offer **P**raise

Make **R**equest

Listen for **A**nswer

Yield to God

1 Timothy 2:8

Notes _____

*The old enemy **Fear** is:*

***F**eeling*

***E**vil*

***A**nxiety*

***R**eturning*

"The Lord is my light and my salvation; whom shall I fear? The Lord is the strength of my life; of whom shall I be afraid?" Psalm 27:1

---

*The old enemy **Fear** is:*

***F**eeling*

***E**vil*

***A**nxiety*

***R**eturning*

Psalm 27:1

Notes

*If you start to **Panic:***

Pray

Acknowledge

Now

Ignore

Crisis

"So he answered, 'Do Not fear, for those who are with us are more than those who are with them.'"
2 Kings 6:16

---

*If you start to **Panic:***

Pray

Acknowledge

Now

Ignore

Crisis

2 Kings 6:16

Notes

When we have a **Problem:**

Pray

Read

Our

Bible

Loosen

Emotional

Misery

"I, Daniel, was grieved in my spirit within my body, and the visions of my head troubled me." Daniel 7:15

When we have a **Problem**

Pray

Read

Our

Bible

Loosen

Emotional

Misery

Daniel 7:15

Notes_____

Satan:

Seducer

Attacking

Thoughts

Actions

Needlessly

"And the Lord said to Satan, 'From where do you come?' So Satan answered the Lord and said, 'From going to and fro on the earth, and from walking back and forth on it.'"
Job 1:7

Satan:

Seducer

Attacking

Thoughts

Actions

Needlessly

Job 1:7

Notes

Devil:

Destructive

Evil

Viciously

Inserting

Lies

"He who sins is of the devil, for the devil has sinned from the beginning. For this purpose the Son of God was manifested, that He might destroy the works of the devil." 1 John 3:8

Devil:

Destructive

Evil

Viciously

Inserting

Lies

1 John 3:8

Notes

Temptation:

Thoughts

Entering

Mind

Playing

Tricks

Accomplish

Tormenting

Individual

Oppressive

Notions

"But the ones on the rock are those who, when they hear, receive the word with joy; and these have no root, who believe for a while and in time of temptation fall away."
Luke 8:13

Temptation:

Thoughts

Entering

Mind

Playing

Tricks

Accomplish

Tormenting

Individual

Oppressive

Notions

Luke 8:13

Notes

*When you **Try** do you:*

Trust God

And **R**emove

Yourself

"Search me, O God, and know my heart; try me, and know my anxieties..." Psalm 139:23

---

*When you **Try** do you:*

Trust God

And

Remove

Yourself

Psalm 139:23

Notes

Fasting *is:*

Fighting

Against

Sin

Turning

Inward

Needing

God

"Then I set my face toward the Lord God to make request by prayer and supplications, with fasting, sackcloth, and ashes." Daniel 9:3

Fasting *is:*

Fighting

Against

Sin

Turning

Inward

Needing

God

Daniel 9:3

Notes

An easy quick prayer **Help:**

Hear

Everything

Lord

Please

"And the Lord shall help them and deliver them; He shall deliver them from the wicked, and save them, because they trust Him."
Psalm 37:40

An easy quick prayer **Help:**

Hear

Everything

Lord

Please

Psalm 37:40

Notes

Worry *is:*

Wondering

On

Revolving

Resolutions

Yourself

"…and to give you who are troubled rest with us when the Lord Jesus is revealed from heaven with His mighty angels…" 2 Thessalonians 1:7

Worry *is:*

Wondering

On

Revolving

Resolutions

Yourself

2 Thessalonians 1:7

Notes

*Do you feel **Broken?***

Believe in God's

Resurrection

Obey God's Word

Keep yourself open for God

Express your feelings to God

Nurture yourself with God's promises

"For He Himself is our peace, who has made both one, and has broken down the middle wall of separation..." Ephesians 2:14

---

*Do you feel **Broken?***

Believe in God's

Resurrection

Obey God's Word

Keep yourself open for God

Express your feeling to God

Nurture yourself with God's promises

Ephesians 2:14

Notes

Rejoice:

Rapturous

Evangelical

Joy

Once

I

Commit

Everything

"…yet I will rejoice in the Lord, I will joy in the God of my salvation."
Habakkuk 3:18

Rejoice:

Rapturous

Evangelical

Joy

Once

I

Commit

Everything

Habakkuk 3:18

Notes_____

Hell is full of:

Horrendous

Evil

Lives

Lost

"Lord, You have heard the desire of the humble; You will prepare their heart; You will cause Your ear to hear, to do justice to the fatherless and the oppressed, that the man of the earth may oppress no more."
Psalm 10:17-18

Hell is full of:

Horrendous

Evil

Lives

Lost

Psalm 10:17-18

Notes

Praise *is a:*

Powerful

Reverent

Abundant

Intense

Spiritual

Expression

"Therefore by Him let us continually offer the sacrifice of praise to God, that is, the fruit of our lips, giving thanks to His name." Hebrews 13:15

Praise *is a:*

Powerful

Reverent

Abundant

Intense

Spiritual

Expression

Hebrews 13:15

Notes

Favor is a gift of:

*F*ree

*A*nointing

*V*astly

*O*verflowing

*R*estoration

"Blessed are those who do His commandments, that they may have the right to the tree of life, and may enter through the gates into the city." Revelation 22:14

Favor is a gift of:

*F*ree

*A*nointing

*V*astly

*O*verflowing

*R*estoration

Revelation 22:14

Notes_____

A **Follower** is:

Faithful

Observant

Loving

Learning

Obeying

Worshipful

Emulating

Redeemed

"Therefore be imitators of God as dear children." Ephesians 5:1

A **Follower** is:

Faithful

Observant

Loving

Learning

Obeying

Worshipful

Emulating

Redeemed

Ephesians 5:1

Notes

Death *is:*

Departing

Earth

And

Touring

Heaven

"We are confident, yes, well pleased rather to be absent from the body and to be present with the Lord."
2 Corinthians 5:8

Death *is:*

Departing

Earth

And

Touring

Heaven

2 Corinthians 5:8

*Notes*_____

God is the great *I Am:*

*I*nvincible

*A*mazing

*M*iraculous

"Remember the former things of old, for I am God…and there is none like Me…" Isaiah 46:9

God is the great *I Am:*

*I*nvincible

*A*mazing

*M*iraculous

Isaiah 46:9

Notes

*Meaning of **Easter:***

Emmanuel dying on

A cross provided

Salvation; offering

The gift of

Eternal life through His

Resurrection

"But he said to them, 'Do not be alarmed. You seek Jesus of Nazareth, who was crucified. He is risen! He is not here. See the place where they laid Him.'" Mark 16:6

---

*Meaning of **Easter:***

Emmanuel dying on

A cross provided

Salvation; offering

The gift of

Eternal life through His

Resurrection

Mark 16:6

*Notes*_____

Thanksgiving:

Time to help others

Health

Answered prayers

Nature

Kindness from strangers

Shared blessings

Guidance from friends

Individual relationships

Victory in Jesus

Insight to see others' needs

Not worrying

God's grace

"...that I may proclaim with the voice of thanksgiving, and tell of all Your wondrous works." Psalm 26:7

Thanksgiving:

Time to help others

Health

Answered prayers

Nature

Kindness from strangers

Shared blessings

Guidance from friends

Individual relationships

Victory in Jesus

Insight to see others' needs

Not worrying

God's grace

Psalm 26:7

Notes

Christmas:

Christ

Helping

Rebellious

Individuals

Sent

To

Mankind

A

Savior

"For there is born to you this day in the city of David a Savior, who is Christ the Lord." Luke 2:11

Christmas

Christ

Helping

Rebellious

Individuals

Sent

To

Mankind

A

Savior

Luke 2:11

Notes

Mercy:

Miracles by God

Eternity with God

Righteousness of God

Compassion from God

YHWH-Shalom (Peace) is God

"...keep yourselves in the love of God, looking for the mercy of our Lord Jesus Christ unto eternal life."
Jude 1:21

Mercy:

Miracles by God

Eternity with God

Righteousness of God

Compassion from God

YHWH-Shalom (Peace) is God

Jude 1:21

Notes

I hope you enjoyed our time together. May the acrostics encourage you along your journey of growth. I am asking God to guide, protect, and comfort you always. Before we part I have a question for you. What would YOU say is God's greatest gift?

Some would say Christmas. Jesus agreed to be born into the world. He lived among mankind for 33 years as our life's example. Christmas is God giving us a savior.

Others would say Easter. At the age of 33 Jesus died for our sins. Easter, the holiday when even secular businesses will close. Easter service is one of the highest spikes in church attendance regardless of denomination. Easter is Jesus enduring our salvation.

I believe that everyone should consider that the greatest gift from God to humanity is Mercy.

Christmas is covered by Mercy. For without sin there would have been no need for a savior to be born. Christmas: Jesus entering the world as a newborn.

Easter is covered by Mercy. Very few if any humans have ever been as vexed in spirit as to sweat drops of blood. Not Jesus' will but God's will be done. God's will is that humans have a way of redemption. What would it cost? What could come close to paying the price of mankind's sin? Only one held such value: God's only son, Jesus. So for God's price to be met, our salvation was purchased by Jesus' enduring death on the cross AND His resurrection from the tomb.

Why would God desire and Jesus agree to fulfill such a plan? MERCY.

Mercy brought me my savior, Jesus. Mercy gave me the gift of redemption through Jesus' resurrection. Mercy covers me every moment of my life. For me God's greatest gift is MERCY.

You can experience salvation and share God's gift of mercy by asking Jesus to be your savior. I would feel privileged to lead you in the following prayer:

"Dear Lord Jesus, come into my heart. I ask you to be my Lord and Savior. I believe you died on the cross for ALL mankind. I believe you rose again on the third day and now reside in heaven. Please forgive me of my sins. I come to you in childlike faith. Help me Lord to grow in your ways. I want to live for you. You said you will not leave me nor forsake me. I take You at Your word. In Jesus' holy name I pray. Amen."

Date I became a child of the King:

_____

If you have a Bible please start to read it. The book of John is a good place to start. If you are not familiar with the Bible, the Living version of the Bible is very easy to understand. If you would like a more in-depth study try an Amplified Bible. Find a Bible-believing, spirit-filled church; they can help you grow.

May life treat you and yours well

May your days be filled with sunshine and happiness

May your rainy days always end with a double rainbow

May God continue to watch over you

www.ingramcontent.com/pod-product-compliance
Lightning Source LLC
Chambersburg PA
CBHW042304150426
43197CB00001B/13